Discovering Mission La Purísima Concepción

BY ZACHARY ANDERSON

Cavendish
Square
New York

Published in 2015 by Cavendish Square Publishing, LLC
243 5th Avenue, Suite 136, New York, NY 10016

CPSIA Compliance Information: Batch #WS14CSQ

All websites were available and accurate when this book was sent to press.

Library of Congress Cataloging-in-Publication Data

Anderson, Zachary.
Discovering Mission La Purísima Concepción / Zachary Anderson.
pages cm. — (California missions)
Includes index.
ISBN 978-1-62713-094-3 (hardcover) ISBN 978-1-62713-096-7 (ebook)
1. Mission La Purísima Concepción (Calif.)—History—Juvenile literature. 2. Spanish mission buildings—California—Lompoc Region—History—Juvenile literature. 3. Franciscans—California—Lompoc Region—History—Juvenile literature. 4. Chumash Indians—Missions—California—Lompoc Region—History—Juvenile literature. 5. California—History—To 1846—Juvenile literature. I. Title.

F869.M65A54 2014
979.4'91—dc23

2014011782

Editorial Director: Dean Miller
Editor: Kristen Susienka
Copy Editor: Cynthia Roby
Art Director: Jeffrey Talbot
Designer: Douglas Brooks
Photo Researcher: J8 MediaProduction Manager: Jennifer Ryder-Talbot
Production Editor: David McNamara

Printed in the United States of America

Contents

Mission La Purísima Concepción is unique from any other California mission because of its formation

1
Exploring a New World

The beautiful California highway *El Camino Real* is dotted with twenty-one centuries-old structures that have a special significance in the history of the state: the missions. Each of these historical sites has its own incredible tale of how it came to be. Mission La Purísima Concepción, known as the Linear Mission for its straight complex of buildings, was the eleventh mission founded. Like the other missions, its past is full of strong beliefs, hard work, and heartache.

SPANIARDS ARRIVE

In the late 1400s and early 1500s, many European countries searched for new land across the waters. Spain was one of the most successful empires during this time. In 1492, Spain's king and queen sent Italian explorer Christopher Columbus west across the sea to find a trade route to Asia. Columbus returned in 1493 with riches, jewels, and captives found not in Asia, however, but in what became known as the **New World**. His stories of what lay beyond the waters encouraged other explorers to follow in his footsteps.

In 1519, a **conquistador** named Hernán Cortés arrived in what is now Mexico. He and his men conquered the Aztec empire living there in 1521. They renamed the Aztec lands "New Spain," officially

Explorers like Hernán Cortés went to the New World to search for treasures, trade routes, and land.

expanding Spain's rule across the Atlantic Ocean. In 1541, explorer Juan Rodríguez Cabrillo sailed to the west coast of New Spain, where he encountered more Native people and lots of land, including the port of San Miguel—but he did not find any riches or jewels. Although Cabrillo died during this journey, his crew continued on, and their maps would guide other explorers for decades.

In 1602, Sebastián Vizcaíno followed Cabrillo's maps and claimed the ports of San Miguel (renamed San Diego) and Monterey for Spain. However, when he, too, returned without the riches Columbus and Cortés had found, Spain decided to stop exploring that part of the world. It was not until 1767 that the country renewed its interest in the land there.

SPAIN TRIES AGAIN

When King Carlos III of Spain learned that Britain and Russia were exploring the California area in the mid-1700s, he appointed Gaspár de Portolá as the governor of Alta California to protect Spain's claim on it. In 1769, Portolá was told to establish settlements in Alta California—an undertaking that would take years of effort from the soldiers and **Franciscan friars** (called *frays* in Spanish) who would dedicate their lives to the task.

2
The Chumash

When the Spanish arrived in *Alta*, or "upper," California, they were greeted by groups of **indigenous people** who had lived there for generations. These groups, or tribes, lived in village communities, each of which was run by a leader called a chief. Each spoke their own language, or dialect of a language, and had their own lifestyle, beliefs, and traditions. The Native tribe most associated with Mission La Purísima Concepción is the Chumash.

HOW THE CHUMASH LIVED

The Chumash lived along the coast of California, from the Santa Monica Mountains to present-day San Luis Obispo. This tribe, which had more than 20,000 members across several villages at the time the Spanish arrived, is believed to have lived there for thousands of years.

The Chumash lived life like many of the other tribes in California did. Men and young boys hunted and fished for food. Women and young girls gathered wild fruits, nuts, and vegetables to store and eat. With natural food abundant, they did not plant and farm any crops.

Each village consisted of family homes, a building for religious ceremonies, and a sweathouse called a *temescal*. Houses were large dome-shaped huts made from thatched reeds and poles, and sometimes whalebone. One house could hold fifty people.

Every Chumash village also had a *shaman*, a religious and medical leader who healed the sick and gave advice. Shamans were also astronomers who mapped the skies. The skies were consulted whenever problems arose, and they helped shamans make important decisions for individuals or for the community.

WHAT MADE THE CHUMASH UNIQUE

There were several things that made the Chumash different from most of the other California tribes. The most important of these differences was their ability to travel on the ocean in boats called

tomols. Unlike the canoes made in other Native communities, tomols were carefully crafted large boats between 12 and 24 feet (3.7 and 7.3 meters) long. Logs were split and shaped into boards, which then had holes drilled into them. The holes were fastened together with red milkweed fiber chords. Any gaps between the boards or the holes were sealed with melted tar that had washed up from the beach. Tomols were often painted red and decorated with seashells. Double-bladed paddles, similar to those used for a kayak, propelled them through the waves.

The Chumash were also known for their excellent weaving skills. They made baskets, bowls, trays, and hats from coiled juncus rush stems or split **tule**. The different colors of these natural materials were used to form beautiful designs on these baskets,

The Chumash were expert boat makers, basket makers, and fishermen.

which were lined inside with a substance to make them water-proof. Water or soup could be boiled in them by heating rocks and putting them inside. Four hundred authentic Chumash baskets have survived, including a large collection at the Santa Barbara Museum of Natural History.

This tribe also left behind paintings in charcoal and in color on the walls of caves. They believed the land was a gift from their creator, and if they respected nature and treated the land with care, it would provide them with everything they needed.

Many Chumash people decorated their bodies with headdresses and paint.

CHUMASH CLOTHING

Men and women dressed differently according to the weather. In warmer months, men and boys wore little or no clothing, while women and girls wore skirts made of deer or animal hide. In colder weather, men wore capes, while women wore animal skins that covered their whole bodies. Both men and women pierced their ears and wore their hair long.

The Chumash's entire way of life changed, however, when the Spanish arrived.

3
The Mission System

When Spain sent Gaspár de Portolá and his expedition into Alta California in 1769, there was already a mission system in place in *Baja*, or "lower," California. Jesuit priests had founded and managed seventeen missions during decades of Spanish rule in that area. In 1767, however, the Jesuits were told to leave the missions, and Franciscan priests took their place instead.

TEACHING THE NATIVE PEOPLE

The goal of the Spanish government was to have the friars in Alta California **convert** Native Americans into Spanish citizens, while the soldiers were to build *presidios*, or forts, to protect the land and the mission communities. The Spanish thought this would be easier than sending settlers into the unknown to start settlements. By teaching the Native people Spanish traditions, language, and beliefs, the Spanish would also have a stronger defense against any countries seeking to claim California's land.

The Franciscan priests considered the Native people "uncivilized" because they worshipped different gods, had their own education style and food-gathering techniques, and wore different types of clothing. As missionaries, the priests saw it as their religious duty to convert the Native communities to Christianity in order to ensure that they would go to heaven.

STARTING THE MISSION SYSTEM

In order to start a mission, the friars first had to get permission from the Spanish **viceroy**. A group of friars and soldiers were then sent to find the perfect piece of land. There were many important things to look for when choosing a mission site: a large area of land inhabited by a Native tribe that featured freshwater, fertile soil, and wooded areas was considered ideal for creating a successful mission.

The Historic Missions, Presidios & Pueblos of California

The Alta California mission system was made up of twenty-one missions and four presidios, established from 1769 to 1823.

San Francisco Solano
San Rafael Arcángel
San Francisco de Asís
San Francisco Presidio
San José
Pueblo de San José de Guadalupe
Santa Clara de Asís
Villa de Branciforte
Santa Cruz
San Juan Bautista
Monterey Presidio
San Carlos Borromeo de Carmelo
Nuestra Señora de la Soledad
San Antonio de Padua
San Miguel Arcángel
San Luis Obispo de Tolosa
La Purísima Concepción
Santa Inés Virgen y Mártir
Santa Bárbara
Santa Bárbara Presidio
San Buenaventura
San Fernando Rey de España
San Gabriel Arcángel
Pueblo of Nuestra Señora de Los Ángeles
San Juan Capistrano
San Luis Rey de Francia
San Diego Presidio
San Diego de Alcalá

Fray Junipero Serra was the first leader of the Alta California missions.

When the friars found a place that suited their needs, a large cross was built where the church would eventually be constructed, and the ground was dedicated to God and to Spain.

JUNÍPERO SERRA

One of the friars who traveled with Portolá in 1769 was Fray Junípero Serra. Serra had come to New Spain from Spain and had successfully converted many Natives in Baja California. He was chosen to be the first president of the California missions, and would supervise Spain's new missions in Alta California. Junípero Serra founded the first Alta California mission, San Diego de Alcalá, during the expedition with Portolá—and others quickly followed. In all, there would be twenty-one missions built between 1769 and 1823

4
Founding the Mission

Fray Junípero Serra founded the first nine missions in Alta California. After his death in 1784 he was replaced by a new president, Fray Fermín Francisco de Lasuén. Fray Lasuén would be responsible for founding La Purísima Concepción in 1787.

CHOOSING A SITE

La Purísima Concepción was originally located in an area the Native people called Algsacpi. The Spanish called it the plain of Río Santa Rosa. A beautiful place surrounded by rolling hills, Fray Lasuén chose the plain of Río Santa Rosa as a mission site for its beauty and its proximity to a Chumash village.

La Purísima Concepción was dedicated on December 8, 1787. Upon his arrival, Fray Lasuén had a temporary shelter built to serve as a church. He then said a Mass and sprinkled **holy water** on the ground, making it known this was sacred area.

It was not until March 1788 that permanent friars arrived at the mission. These men were named Vicente Fustér and José Arroita. Vicente Fustér had worked at other missions in Alta California before his arrival at La Purísima Concepción, including San Diego de Alcalá, San Gabriel Arcángel, and San Juan Capistrano. He was familiar with conversions and speaking to Native people, which made him valuable to the mission's plan to **baptize** them as members of the Christian faith. A Native person who accepted Christianity and came to live at the mission was called a **neophyte**. The neophytes helped build the mission's many buildings while learning Spanish ways.

NEOPHYTES

One of the first things the friars did was translate both the Mass ceremony and a book of Catholic teachings, called a catechism, into the Chumash language. It was hoped that with these translations available, the friars would have more success bringing the Chumash to Christianity. However, the first years of the mission attracted few converts. Frightened by the Spanish and their strange ways and weapons, some members of the Chumash tribe fled to other parts of California. Others feared that becoming a neophyte would mean losing their own culture and made a conscious decision to stay away from the mission.

Before joining the mission, a neophyte had to be baptized into the Catholic faith—not always an easy task for the friars.

The young and curious, however, were attracted to La Purísima Concepción. They were interested in the skills the friars offered to teach them in exchange for listening to their ideas about God and for their help in building the mission. Before long, more neophytes joined the mission and the population grew.

BUILDING THE MISSION

Soon after their arrival, the friars and the soldiers began constructing temporary structures. The first structure built was the church, followed by friars' living quarters, barracks for the soldiers that would live there, a granary, a kitchen, and an

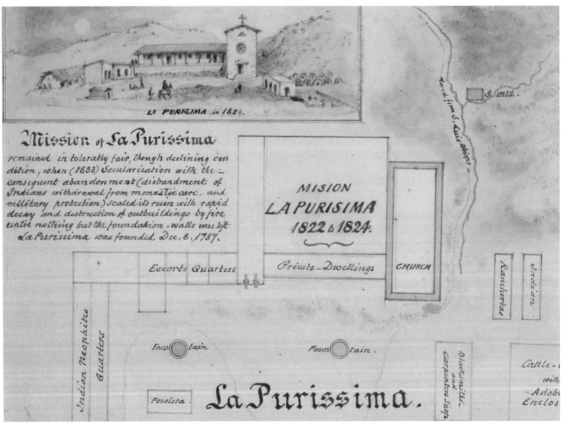

This ground plan and sketch of the mission from 1824 gives an idea of what the mission was like then.

infirmary. As with most of the California missions, all of Mission La Purísima Concepción's buildings were laid out in a square shape called a **quadrangle**. This shape made the mission more likely to be protected in the event of an attack.

These temporary buildings were constructed from local resources such as wood, branches, and brush. When Native people joined the community, they were taught to make sturdier **adobe**

Techniques used by the neophytes to make adobe bricks are used today.

bricks to construct the permanent buildings that replaced the temporary ones. To make adobe, the neophytes mixed mud, straw, and water with their bare feet. Then they shaped the mixture with their hands into bricks that would bake in the sun.

BUILDING THE MISSION CHURCH

Mission La Purísima Concepción's first church was built in 1789. Made of adobe bricks, the roof of the church was flat and covered with straw. The missionaries and neophytes used this church until 1798, when the mission's population had grown to 920 people. The existing church was no longer large enough to hold everyone, so the neophytes built a new and better one under the direction of the friars.

LIFE AT THE MISSION

While the first few years at Mission La Purísima Concepción were very successful, life was becoming more difficult for the Chumash who chose not to join the mission. They found their old ways disrupted by the Spanish settlements taking over the land, the cattle destroying the water holes and plants that they had depended on to survive, and the people from other countries who hunted otter illegally. Many of these Native people, frustrated and running out of options, eventually moved to the mission as well. By 1804, more than 1,520 neophytes lived and worked at Mission La Purísima Concepción.

That same year, a new friar, Fray Mariano Payéras, arrived. He taught the neophytes how to tend peas, beans, peaches, olives, and corn, and how to build an **irrigation** system that brought water to the mission. Likewise, he encouraged the neophytes to trade with the settlers coming to build *pueblos*, or towns, nearby.

The pueblo of Los Angeles was one of the major trading places for La Purísima Concepción.

5
Early Days at the Mission

Fray Payéras brought much success to Mission La Purísima Concepción, but he could not prevent problems from arising. In 1804, a smallpox epidemic struck. The Native people had not developed immunity to European illnesses, and between 1804 and 1807, about 500 neophytes died. Frightened by what they saw, other neophytes began to leave.

Sickness was not the only reason the Chumash fled. Mission life was regimented, and many Native people struggled to follow the rules. Neophytes were not allowed to practice their Chumash customs and traditions, and were often forced against their will to stay within the confines of La Purísima Concepción. Those caught trying to escape were punished, often by being flogged, or whipped.

EARTHQUAKES

In 1812, a series of natural disasters struck that left the mission devastated. Many earthquakes shook throughout California that year, the worst one occurring on December 21, at 10:30 a.m. The mission shook for four minutes, and when it stopped, it was clear that the buildings had been affected—some of them badly. Several aftershocks followed, further damaging the work the missionaries and neophytes had done. After the earthquakes came severe rainstorms that caused a massive flood, exposing clay and washing away whole structures.

Thanks to the earthquakes and the flood, the mission wasn't much more than a few walls rising out of a muddy puddle. The neophytes thought it was a bad omen, and many of them refused to stay at the mission site. Fray Payéras requested to move the mission to a new location, 4.5 miles (7.2 kilometers) northeast of the original site.

A NEW LOCATION

As soon as they received permission from the officials in New Spain, the friars, soldiers, neophytes, and other community members abandoned what was left of the original mission grounds and headed north to a canyon called *La Cañada de los Berros*, which means "The Canyon of the Watercress." The soil there was very rich and fertile. There was a lot of water available from nearby springs, and because the area was sheltered, the winds were never very strong.

The first site of Mission La Purísima Concepción, near the city of Lompoc, is still visible today, though its buildings are mostly rubble.

BUILDING THE NEW MISSION

The friars were afraid of another earthquake, so special measures were taken during construction of the new Mission La Purísima Concepción. Most significantly, the buildings for the new

Some materials from the old mission site were used to build the new mission.

mission were laid out in a straight line. The friars believed that this new design would make it easier for people to escape if another earthquake hit. The second Mission La Purísima Concepción—sometimes called the Linear Mission—was the only one of the twenty-one California missions that was not built in the traditional quadrangle style.

To make the new buildings stronger, the friars instructed the neophytes to make the walls four feet (1.2 m) thick, and to use stone columns to reinforce them. The friars also salvaged and repurposed materials from the original mission and incorporated them into the new one.

THE MISSION COMPLEX

The first building to go up in the new location was a temporary church, which was capable of serving more than 1,000 people. Later, a church made of adobe bricks replaced it.

When the neophytes finished the main residence building in 1815, it had rooms for the friars to live in, guest rooms, offices, a store, dining rooms, and a small church.

A cemetery was built next to the church. Historical records show that hundreds of people were buried there. It became the official church cemetery in 1821.

ADDITIONAL MISSION BUILDINGS

There were other important buildings at the mission. A gristmill—a machine that grinds corn and wheat to make flour—was located just north of the church. The gristmill was run by a *burro*, or donkey. The burro walked in a circle, causing a grinding wheel to turn. There was also a kitchen where food was prepared, and rooms for weaving, making soap, blacksmithing, and other skills.

A springhouse was set a little farther away from the blacksmith's shop and was very important at Mission La Purísima Concepción. This stone building was where the water from the nearby springs was filtered. The filtered water then ran underground to the areas of the mission where freshwater was needed, such as the central fountain. The mission also had a tank to store water.

HOUSING

As in the original mission, the friars lived in the main residence building, while the neophytes lived in a long adobe structure not far away. The neophytes' homes were called *rancherías*.

Married couples lived in long buildings of two-room apartments, where they could raise their small children. However, the friars did not want neophytes teaching their older children the Native way of life, so as soon as they were old enough, they were separated from their parents. Girls over the age of eleven were sent to live and work in *monjeríos* with the other unmarried women in the mission. This dormitory was locked at night when they went to bed. Boys were sent to sleep in the mission hallways with the other unmarried men.

6
Daily Life at the Mission

After a Native person became a Christian and dedicated their lives to Mission La Purísima Concepción, they had to follow a strict schedule of prayer, work, and rest. The Spanish friars believed that discipline was an important part of becoming a good Christian, and all missions followed similar patterns from day to day.

THE MISSION SCHEDULE

In 1800, the friars in charge submitted a report that outlined daily life at Mission La Purísima Concepción. The report stated that neophytes did not work more than five hours a day, and were also allowed some time to leave the mission and visit their tribe. However, the friars who took charge after 1800 changed this initial schedule over the years, enforcing longer work hours and more restrictions.

A typical day at Mission La Purísima Concepción started around sunrise. A bell tolled to signal it was time to wake, and everyone headed to the church to pray. After prayer, breakfast was served. The Chumash men and women then went to work, and the children stayed behind for religious instruction by the friars.

The women were in charge of preparing the food for the mission community. They learned how to make many Spanish dishes while incorporating techniques and tools they had used before, such as a mortar and pestle to grind up food. They were also taught how to make candles, soap, and clothing. They wove on large looms rather than entirely by hand, as they had done in their Native villages.

Instead of hunting, as they had done in the past, the men worked at the mission using new skills such as leatherworking, woodcraft, farming, and blacksmithing that they'd been taught by the friars and other experts from New Spain.

At noon each day, the neophytes ate lunch. They did not eat the acorns or plants they were used to eating. Instead, they had either a vegetable or meat stew called *pozole*, or a cornmeal soup called *atole*. After lunch they enjoyed a rest period called a *siesta*. After a siesta, everyone worked for a few more hours until dusk, when it was time for evening prayers and dinner. The women went to bed around 8 p.m. and the men around 9 p.m.

This plaque in Sacramento recognizes the mission's founding in 1787.

THE LANGUAGE

According to the mission report of 1800, everyone at Mission La Purísima Concepción was encouraged to learn to speak a type of Spanish called Castilian. This language originated in the northern and central regions of Spain and is still spoken today. Even though the friars taught the language to the neophytes, many of them spoke a combination of Castilian and Native words.

CROPS AND LIVESTOCK

Along with learning a new language at Mission La Purísima Concepción, neophytes were taught how to farm crops such as wheat, barley, corn, and lentils. These crops were very important to running the mission, as they provided the mission with food and other products to sell to the pueblos, presidios, and ranches nearby. The neophytes were also responsible for tending the mission's large vineyards and olive orchards, as well as for making the wine and olive oil.

To water the crops and provide the mission population with water to drink and bathe, the friars and soldiers instructed neophytes to build an irrigation system. This system brought water from nearby springs through a series of pipes to the springhouse on the mission grounds, where it was filtered for use.

Livestock such as cows and sheep provided the community with food and the materials to make warm clothing. In 1822, Mission La Purísima Concepción recorded having 23,746 animals—the largest number of livestock in its existence. Each animal was marked with the mission's own specific brand, or design, to identify them as mission property and make it easier to count them. Neophytes and soldiers were responsible for taking

Both the original mission (its ruins pictured above) and the new location had fields for cattle to graze and rich soil for growing crops.

care of the animals. Through careful instruction, neophytes learned how to ride small, fast horses and became expert cowboys, called *vaqueros*. To keep the herds safe, neophytes also learned how to control weapons such as guns.

MISSION HEADQUARTERS

In 1815, Fray Payéras was promoted to mission president. Rather than move to the previous mission headquarters, San Carlos Borroméo del Río Carmelo, however, Fray Payéras chose to stay at Mission La Purísima Concepción. He was the mission's longest-serving friar, living and working there for nineteen years until his death in 1823. Fray Payéras was buried underneath the church altar, and will always be remembered for his special role in the history of the mission.

7
Troubled Times

Despite the new opportunities granted to the Chumash people at Mission La Purísima Concepción, many were unhappy. In the early 1800s, before Fray Payéras arrived, the friars and soldiers at the mission were said to have treated the neophytes very badly, hurting them and punishing them. This treatment worsened between 1810 and 1821, when New Spain and Spain were at war. These problems led to one of the worst incidents in Mission La Purísima Concepción's history since the earthquake of 1812.

CHANGING TIMES

In 1810, political change began to take shape when some of New Spain's citizens wanted the country to break free from Spain's rule. The Spanish government had controlled the lands for centuries, however, and had no intention of giving in to those people who challenged them. From 1810 to 1821, the war for New Spain's independence gripped the country.

The conflict was particularly hard on the missions of Alta California. Spain had previously supplied the friars with resources to survive. This included a small living allowance for the priests that came from the Pious Fund—a collection of money from the faithful that was distributed to each mission. Those in support of New Spain's independence blocked off supply routes, preventing Spain from sending these supplies to the missions.

The salaries for the soldiers were also paid by the Spanish government. After 1810, however, the money for the soldiers had to go instead to supporting Spain's efforts to win two wars: the conflict in New Spain and another war with France. Many soldiers living at the missions were paid very little to begin with, and this new turn of events angered them very much. Soon, they began taking their anger out on the neophytes.

A CHAIN REACTION

While many of the friars chose to live at the missions, the soldiers were ordered to live there by the Spanish government. It was their job to keep order, protect mission life, and punish those who broke mission rules. Some soldiers took advantage of the neophytes. If they didn't get their salary from the government, they might take food, clothing, or other goods from the neophytes. Sometimes the soldiers would unjustly flog them. All of this added to the tension between the converted Chumash and the Spanish.

In 1824, a neophyte from Mission La Purísima Concepción visited a relative who was imprisoned at Mission Santa Inés, about twenty miles away. During the visit, a Santa Inés soldier whipped the La Purísima neophyte. This caused an uproar from the neophytes at Mission Santa Inés. They attacked the soldiers, burned down several buildings, and took control of Mission Santa Inés.

News of the revolt reached Mission La Purísima Concepción very quickly. The Chumash neophytes there immediately turned against the La Purísima Concepción soldiers.

UPRISING

The neophytes took their revenge against the soldiers for how they had been treated. They did not want to harm the friars, however. While they took the soldiers' guns and stole their horses, they also informed the friars that they could leave. Two of the friars left, while one chose to stay.

Some neophytes fled the mission and took cover in the hills nearby. Others remained and held the mission, and kept watch for any suspected trespassers. Four Mexican travelers were killed by neophytes during the panic that night.

The mission soldiers barricaded themselves in their living quarters and eventually surrendered. The neophytes controlled Mission La Purísima Concepción for almost a month, holding the soldiers prisoner.

On March 16, 1824, Mexican soldiers arrived to suppress the uprising. The soldiers attacked, and in the two-and-a-half-hour battle, sixteen neophytes and one soldier were killed. After surrendering, seven neophytes were executed for having killed the Mexican travelers on the first night of the rebellion. Twelve others were sentenced to hard labor at the presidio in Monterey. To prevent another revolt, the remaining neophytes at Mission La Purísima Concepción found their freedom would become even more suppressed.

AFTERMATH

Some of the neophytes who had fled during the riot had enjoyed living at the mission, and were relieved to return after the revolt.

After uprisings at the mission, some people left to find better lives. Many became *vaqueros* at ranches nearby.

Other neophytes, however, were still unhappy with their situation, and returned to Mission La Purísima Concepción only because they had nowhere else to go. By this time, many Chumash traditions were lost to the neophytes. It was almost impossible for them to remember Native ways, or to find a Native group to join if they left the mission. Many Native groups had moved elsewhere in California, or had been entirely absorbed into the mission system. Neophytes who did leave usually worked in the pueblos or on ranches as vaqueros.

By the mid-twentieth century, the Chumash language and way of life was almost completely forgotten. Only in recent years have linguists—people who speak and study many languages—come together to study the Chumash people. Descendants still live on to this day, but many do not speak the language of their ancestors. With the help of these linguists, the Chumash language is being resurrected and taught in classrooms around California.

8
Secularization

Following eleven years of civil war with Spain, New Spain, now called Mexico, won its independence in 1821. With independence came big changes for the California mission system.

DIVIDING THE LAND

The Mexican government knew that most of the rich and fertile land in Alta California was owned by the missions. They wanted to take control of the missions away from the Catholic Church and divide the land between government and military figures, settlers, and the Native people. This process was called **secularization**. The missions would be made into pueblos and ranches for settlers, and the only religious buildings that would remain were the churches, which would be run by priests from Mexico. All of the Spanish friars and those soldiers loyal to Spain had to leave.

In 1834, this plan was put into action. Originally it was decided to hand the majority of the land back to the Native people to run as farms. However, this did not happen. Unfamiliar with the process, many ex-neophytes were cheated out of it by Mexican authorities who wanted the land for themselves.

LOSING THE MISSION LAND

Mission La Purísima Concepción was secularized in 1834. After six months, over half of the mission's property found its way into the hands of Mexican citizens.

Many ex-neophytes found that they could not make a living off the small pieces of land they were given. The old villages that had once belonged to the Chumash were now home to Mexican settlers. With few options available, the Chumash went into the settlements and ranches looking for work, or left the area entirely.

In 1845, control of the mission was entirely removed from the Catholic Church. It was sold in an auction to a man named John Temple, who did not take care of it. Although Mission La Purísima Concepción was given back to the Catholic Church in 1874, it fell into ruin. In 1903, it was bought by the Union Oil Company. They handed it over to the Civilian Conservation Corps, who played a big part in restoring the mission to its former beauty.

After secularization, many neophytes were forced to leave the missions and faced even greater hardships than they experienced while still living there.

9 The Mission Alive Today

The Civilian Conservation Corps (CCC) was a government agency that created civic projects to provide work to unemployed men during the Great Depression. This agency was given permission in the 1930s to restore Mission La Purísima Concepción and make it into an honored historical landmark. A total of 507 acres (207 hectares) of land had been donated for the project by such organizations as the Catholic Church, the Union Oil Company (who owned the mission complex, including the site of the priests' living area), and the State of California. This was a historical as well as architectural project, so the CCC had to study the writings, paintings, and drawings of the mission before they could begin work on the actual restoration.

RESTORING THE MISSION

Restoration work began in 1933. The CCC used many of the same techniques the Native people, soldiers, and friars had used to build the original structures. They dried adobe bricks in the sun, followed the original design of the post-1812 mission, and used tools similar to the ones neophytes would have used. On December 7, 1941, Mission La Purísima Concepción was officially recognized and dedicated as a State Historical Monument.

THE MODERN MISSION

Today Mission La Purísima Concepción is the most completely reconstructed of the twenty-one missions of California. Ten of the original buildings have been restored and furnished to look as they did in 1820. Project workers planted the garden with the same types of plants that grew in the 1800s, and the mission still has the original aqueduct and water system. If you visit today, you will even see the same types of animals that lived there. Unlike other mission churches, however, Mission La Purísima Concepción's church is not active.

Many students and tourists visit Mission La Purísima Concepción every year. In 1973, volunteers formed a group called Prelado de los Tesoros, which means "Keeper of the Treasures." These volunteers run the mission and play the roles of the people who once lived there. You can make candles with them, tour the grounds, or learn how to weave on Spanish looms.

The story of Mission La Purísima Concepción, together with the stories of the other missions, is a critical piece of California's history. While the mission system changed the Native way of life for thousands of indigenous people—which should never be forgotten—it also helped make California a thriving center of agriculture and Spanish design today.

10
Make Your Own Mission Model

**To make your own model of the
La Purísima Concepción mission, you will need:**

- Foam Core board
- paint (green, pink)
- X-ACTO® knife
  (ask an adult to help)
- scissors
- ruler
- pencil
- toothpicks
- tape
- cardboard
- glue
- red construction paper
- imitation grass
- miniature flowers/trees

DIRECTIONS

**Adult supervision
is suggested.**

Step 1: Cut a piece of Foam Core
to 30"× 20" (76.2 cm × 50.8 cm) for
the base of your model. Paint the
base green and let dry.

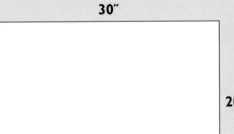

30″

20″

Step 2: To make the side walls of the courtyard, cut two pieces of Foam Core that measure 16"× 2" (40.6 cm × 5.1 cm).

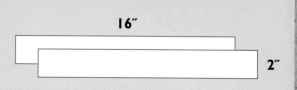

Step 3: To make the end wall of the courtyard, cut a piece of Foam Core board that measures 5.5"× 2" (14 cm × 5.1 cm).

Step 4: To form the courtyard, stick toothpicks into the bottoms of the walls and stick into the Foam Core board base. Tape the walls at the corners.

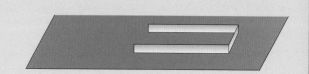

Step 5: To make the church walls, cut out two Foam Core board pieces that measure 12"× 2.5" (30.5 cm × 6.4 cm).

Step 6: Cut two Foam Core board pieces in the shape of a house, 5.5"× 4.5" (14 cm × 11.4 cm). The top should be triangular, so it slopes like a roof. The peak of the roof should be off-center.

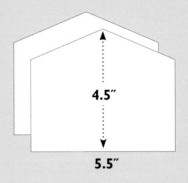

Step 7: Put toothpicks in the bottoms of the church walls and insert into the base. Tape the corners inside the church so the walls stay together.

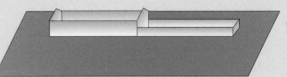

Step 8: Make the bell tower by cutting a piece of Foam Core board that measures 2.5"× 5.5" (6.4 cm × 14 cm).

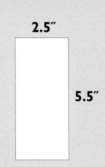

Step 9: Cut three bell windows out with an X-ACTO knife. Cut the top of the tower in the shape of a dome. With toothpicks, stick the tower onto the base.

Step 10: Paint the mission walls pink. To make the church roof, cut a piece of cardboard that measures 14"× 3" (35.6 cm × 7.6 cm). Cut another piece that measures 14"× 4.5" (35.6 cm × 11.4 cm).

Step 11: Glue the cardboard panels on top of the church. Let dry.

Step 12: To make the red tile roof, fold a piece of red construction paper back and forth for a ripple effect. Cut to make it fit both sides of the roof. Glue to the top of the roof.

Step 13: Cut very thin strips of red construction paper and glue them to the tops of the courtyard walls.

Step 14: Decorate the mission grounds with imitation grass, miniature trees, and flowers.

The completed model of Mission La Purísima Concepción.

Key Dates in Mission History

1492   Christopher Columbus reaches the West Indies

1542   Cabrillo's expedition to California

1602   Sebastián Vizcaíno sails to California

1713   Fray Junípero Serra is born

1769   Founding of San Diego de Alcalá

1770   Founding of San Carlos Borroméo del Río Carmelo

1771   Founding of San Antonio de Padua and San Gabriel Arcángel

1772   Founding of San Luis Obispo de Tolosa

1775–76   Founding of San Juan Capistrano

1776   Founding of San Francisco de Asís

1776   Declaration of Independence is signed

1777	Founding of Santa Clara de Asís
1782	Founding of San Buenaventura
1784	Fray Serra dies
1786	Founding of Santa Bárbara
1787	Founding of La Purísima Concepción
1791	Founding of Santa Cruz and Nuestra Señora de la Soledad
1797	Founding of San José, San Juan Bautista, San Miguel Arcángel, and San Fernando Rey de España
1798	Founding of San Luis Rey de Francia
1804	Founding of Santa Inés
1817	Founding of San Rafael Arcángel
1823	Founding of San Francisco Solano
1833	Mexico passes Secularization Act
1848	Gold found in northern California
1850	California becomes the thirty-first state

Glossary

adobe (uh-DOH-bee) Sun-dried bricks made of straw, mud, and sometimes manure.

baptize (BAP-tize) To perform a ceremony when someone is accepted into, or accepts, the Christian faith.

conquistador (kon-KEE-stuh-dor) A Spanish explorer that conquered land for Spain.

convert (kun-VERT) To change religious beliefs.

Franciscan (fran-SIS-kin) A member of a communal Roman Catholic order of friars, or brothers, who follow the teachings and examples of Saint Francis of Assisi, who did much work as a missionary.

friar (FRY-ur) A brother in a communal religious order. Friars can also be priests.

holy water (HO-lee WA-ter) Water that is blessed by a Catholic priest and used for religious ceremonies.

indigenous people (in-DIJ-en-us PEA-pel) People native born to a particular region or environment.

irrigation (eer-ih-GAY-shun) A system devised to supply an area with water.

neophyte (NEE-oh-fyt) The name for an indigenous person baptized into the Christian faith.

New World (NOO WURLD) What the Europeans once called the combined areas of South America, Central America, and North America.

quadrangle (KWAH-drayn-gul) The square at the center of a mission that is surrounded by four buildings.

secularization (seh-kyoo-lur-ih-ZAY-shun) A process by which the mission lands were made to be nonreligious.

tule (TOO-lee) Tightly woven reeds used by the Chumash to help build their homes.

viceroy (VYS-roy) The governor of a place who rules as a representative of the king.

Pronunciation Guide

atole (ah-TOH-lay)

El Camino Real (EL kah-MEE-noh RAY-al)

fray (FRAY)

monjerío (mohn-hay-REE-oh)

pozole (poh-SOH-lay)

pueblos (PWAY-blohz)

siesta (see-EHS-tah)

temescal (TEH-mes-cal)

tomol (TOH-mul)

Find Out More

For more information on Mission La Purísima Concepción and the California missions, check out these books and websites:

BOOKS

Bibby, Brian. *The Fine Art of California Indian Basketry.* Berkeley, CA: Heydey, 2013.

Hicks, Terry Allan. *First Americans: The Chumash.* New York, NY: Cavendish Square, 2008.

Padelsky, Londie. *California Missions.* Ketchum, ID: Stoecklein Publishing, 2006.

Rosinsky, Natalie M. *California Ranchos.* Capstone: Edina, MN, 2006.

Weber, Matt. *California's Missions A to Z.* San Francisco, CA: 121 Publications, 2010.

WEBSITES

California Mission Foundation

www.californiamissionfoundation.org

This website provides historical facts on the missions, as well as current information on the organization that preserves and protects the missions today.

California Missions Resource Center

www.missionscalifornia.com

This is a website that provides great resources on all the California missions.

Chumash Nation Website

www.chumashindian.com

This website outlines a brief history of the Chumash Nation.

La Purísima Mission

www.lapurisimamission.org

This is the official website for the mission landmark today

Website for the Santa Inez Band of Indians

www.santaynezchumash.org/culture.html

This website provides information about the history of the Chumash people.

Index